DR. ALBERT "ACE" GOERIG

THE SECRETS TO
MAXIMIZING
DIVIDEND STOCK
RETURNS

For information about this title or to order other books and/or electronic media, contact the publisher:
ACG Press
222 Lilly Rd. NE, Olympia, WA 98506
DoctorAce.com

ISBNs:
979-8-9880408-6-6 (print)
979-8-9880408-9-7 (eBook)

Printed in the United States of America
Cover and Interior Design: 1106 Design

TABLE OF CONTENTS

Go to www.doctorace.com/ to quickly access links to all the online resources that are referenced in this book.

About the Author

D r. Albert "Ace" Goerig graduated from Case Western Reserve University Dental School and is a retired Army colonel. For the past twenty-seven years he has been both a business and a financial coach to many doctors. In 2004, he wrote his first book: *Time and Money: Your Guide to Personal and Financial Freedom*. His newest books, entitled: *The How-To Book on Dividend Growth Investing—Create Generational Wealth and Passive Income for Life!* published in March 2023 and *The Big Little Book on Creating Personal and Financial Freedom* in June 2024. He has a free website, www.doctorace.com, with audios and videos to help individuals quickly become debt-free and understand simple and safe investing.

Disclaimer

Nothing in the market can be guaranteed. Therefore, it bears repeating here: This guide is for informational and educational purposes only, based on the personal experience and research of the author. Information has been obtained from data sources considered to be reliable, but its accuracy and completeness are not guaranteed. This guide is offered with the understanding that the author and publisher are neither fiduciaries nor engaged in rendering legal, tax, investment, financial, or other advice. All content is general in nature, and your unique circumstances may include factors not considered by the author.

You assume sole responsibility for evaluating the merits and risks of the provided content, as well as that of any third-party websites, providers, or resources mentioned by the author. It is recommended that you conduct appropriate due diligence and consult with professional advisors. The author and publisher specifically disclaim any liability or loss arising from your use, application, or interpretation, directly or indirectly, of any information herein or any referenced third-party resource.

Introduction

When selecting dividend companies, many investors focus on getting high dividend yields along with companies that have a long history of paying dividends. This philosophy has led to long-term mediocre results because they are looking at the wrong numbers. The most important numbers to focus on are the total annual equity return of the company over time and dividend growth. This book will show you a step-by-step approach to maximize your overall returns with your dividend stocks.

It is better to buy a company that has a 1% dividend yield, where your investment of $10,000 grows to $100,000 over 10 years, compared to a company that has a 4% dividend yield, but your $10,000 grows only to $15,000 over the same 10 years. Most of the higher-yield dividend companies that have a dividend yield greater than 2.5% have a total 10-year overall return lower than the S&P 500. Many of these companies are not strong and only use dividends to attract and keep investors. This book focuses on how to find those dividend-paying companies that beat the S&P 500 while providing an annual equity return greater than 15%.

The next important number is to find those companies that meet the first criterion but also have a high dividend-growth rate that consistently increases their dividends every year, even in down markets. We are looking at companies with a proven track record of raising their yearly dividend by 10% or more year after year. High-quality dividend-growth companies typically dominate their industry, realizing steady profits and generating massive amounts of free cash flow. As a result, they're able to pay their shareholders from that cash in the form of a dividend that increases every year.

The beauty of owning a stock like this is that no matter what happens to its share price, if the company continues to grow its dividend, then we—as shareholders—stand to collect larger and larger payouts each year. That's why these stocks are so compelling: you buy them when they're trading at an undervalued price, hold them, and then get showered with growing cash payouts for potentially decades to come!

This book will show you how to find and select the best dividend stocks, give you specific examples of some of the best dividend companies, maximize your returns, minimize your taxes, and receive a never-ending, ever-increasing flow of passive income. This becomes your new low-taxed pension plan for retirement without government control. As the great investor Warren Buffett said, "If you don't find a way to make money while you sleep, you will work until you die."

To do this, I will incorporate much of what I have written in my newest books entitled: *The How-To Book on Dividend Growth Investing—Create Generational Wealth and Passive Income for Life!* published in March 2023 and *The Big Little Book on Creating Personal and Financial Freedom* in June 2024.

Understand the Financial Game

Most Americans do not understand personal finance, the consequences of debt, or how to invest in the stock market. This mindset only helps the financial institutions profit from their fear of managing their money. The majority of those who invest on their own feel overwhelmed by the noise of Wall Street and are ruled by fear and greed, resulting in mediocre returns from their investment strategies.

Most novice investors buy when the price is high and sell when the price is low. They end up sitting on the sidelines during peak surges in the market. They have other bad habits such as trying to get rich overnight, giving their money to someone else to invest, over-diversifying their money, panic selling, and impatience.

Research done by Dalbar, Inc., a company that studies investor behavior and analyzes investor market returns, consistently shows that the average investor earns well-below-average S&P 500 returns.

They are obsessed with the daily information about the stock market. These speculators spend too much time watching or reading investment news and trying to analyze investments. They think they can time and beat the market, while less than 10% of professional fund managers can even beat the S&P 500 over a 3-year period. This strategy increases taxes and fees and gobbles up profits over time.

From January 2000 through December 2021, the S&P 500 Index averaged 7.35% a year, with dividends reinvested each year. During the same period, the average equity-fund investor earned a market return of only 4.25% per year. The reason for the discrepancy in returns is that the average investor loses money through advisory and mutual-fund fees and, influenced by their emotions, jumps in and out of the market,

These individuals are vulnerable to investment schemes and high-fee advisers and brokers. We seem to have an infinite capacity to stress ourselves and do stupid things, especially when it comes to money. To a large degree, this comes from greed, ego, and family encoding.

I knew one individual who took his entire retirement plan of $300,000 and put it into a real-estate limited partnership. He did not understand the potential risks and rewards, and he had no control over it. Within one year, he had lost his entire retirement nest egg, which had taken him 20 years to earn. Another very smart and skilled colleague got involved in a Bernie Madoff-type Ponzi scheme and lost his entire savings of $1.3 million, which had taken him 25 years to accumulate.

The average American's stock market investments are in 401(k) and pension plans. The majority of these investments are in actively managed mutual funds that do not do as well as the S&P 500. These plans rely upon money managers, financial advisers, and brokers who may engage in hyperactive trading to try to beat the market by picking winners and timing. This is a losing strategy. In most cases, investors would be better off consistently investing on their own in an S&P 500 index fund such as (SWPPX).

The Cost of Advisers

Below is a real example of an actively managed mutual-fund simple IRA compared to the results of the S&P 500 fund over 14 years. In this true example, the individual would have had $706,000 rather than $342,000 (more than twice as much) if they would have just put their investments in the S&P 500 ETF (exchange traded fund).

The next real-life example is of a much larger office that maximized all tax-deductible strategies. On the left is the true account invested by their financial adviser in mutual funds. On the right is the result if they had invested on their own in the S&P 500 index fund, with an expense ratio of 0.03%. Just by investing on their own in the S&P 500, this would have had an annual 12.6% return with an ending balance in 2024 of more than $8.3 million in their 401(k) account. Compare this to their financial adviser's management

YEAR	BROKERAGE ACCOUNT $ OPEN BAL	$ DEPOSITS	$ PRINCIPAL	RETURNS %	$	S&P 500 ACCOUNT $ OPEN BAL	$ DEPOSITS	$ PRINCIPAL	RETURNS % PRETAX	$ TREATED
2009	0	7,800	7,800	-0.81%	-63	0	7,800	7,800	26.46%	2,064
2010	7,737	14,950	22,687	5.98%	1,357	9,864	14,950	24,814	15.06%	3,737
2011	24,044	15,400	39,444	-2.44%	-963	28,551	15,400	43,951	2.11%	927
2012	38,481	14,950	53,431	9.99%	5,339	44,878	14,950	59,828	16.00%	9,573
2013	58,770	15,600	74,370	8.56%	6,368	69,401	15,600	85,001	32.39%	27,532
2014	80,738	15,750	96,488	2.86%	2,761	112,532	15,750	128,282	13.69%	17,562
2015	99,249	15,600	114,849	-4.34%	-4,984	145,844	15,600	161,444	1.38%	2,228
2016	109,865	16,900	126,765	6.95%	8,807	163,672	16,900	180,572	11.96%	21,596
2017	135,572	18,650	154,222	12.64%	19,499	202,169	18,650	220,819	21.83%	48,205
2018	173,721	15,654	189,375	-7.26%	-13,751	269,023	15,654	284,677	-4.38%	-12,469
2019	175,624	17,046	192,670	16.67%	32,112	272,209	17,046	289,255	31.49%	91,086
2020	224,782	19,520	244,302	11.24%	27,449	380,341	19,520	399,861	18.40%	73,574
2021	271,751	20,822	292,573	9.37%	27,427	473,435	20,822	494,257	28.71%	141,901
2022	320,000	21,076	341,076	-16.62%	-56,676	636,158	21,076	657,234	-18.11%	-119,025
2023	284,400	21,542	305,942	11.93%	36,503	538,209	21,542	559,751	26.26%	146,991
2024	342,445		342,445			706,742		706,742		

of their portfolio resulting in an annual 7% return with a final balance of $4.25 million. Over the past 12 years, the plan lost more than $4.05 million (almost half) by allowing their financial advisers to manage their investments. The individual just now retired at age 65 and wishes he could go back 12 years and take control of his money back then. We need to learn how to invest safely on our own.

YEAR	BROKERAGE ACCOUNT $ OPEN BAL	$ DEPOSITS	$ PRINCIPAL	RETURNS %	$ GROWTH	S&P 500 ACCOUNT $ OPEN BAL	$ DEPOSITS	$ PRINCIPAL	RETURNS % PRETAX	$ GROWTH
2009	0	0	0			0	0		26.46%	#VALUE!
2010	0	0	0		768,319	0	0		15.06%	#VALUE!
2011	768,319	100,666	868,985	1.33%	11,596	768,319	100,666	868,985	2.11%	18,336
2012	880,581	105,482	986,063	7.97%	78,592	887,321	105,482	992,803	16.00%	158,848
2013	1,064,655	109,001	1,173,656	7.15%	83,897	1,151,651	109,001	1,260,652	32.39%	408,325
2014	1,257,553	120,592	1,378,145	6.80%	93,676	1,668,977	120,592	1,789,569	13.69%	244,992
2015	1,471,821	121,898	1,593,719	-5.96%	-94,920	2,034,561	121,898	2,156,459	1.38%	29,759
2016	1,498,799	424,999	1,923,798	1.25%	24,090	2,186,218	424,999	2,611,217	11.96%	312,302
2017	1,947,888	109,166	2,057,054	17.16%	352,940	2,923,519	109,166	3,032,685	21.83%	662,035
2018	2,409,994	102,891	2,512,885	-7.10%	-178,321	3,694,720	102,891	3,797,611	-4.38%	-166,335
2019	2,334,564	104,551	2,439,115	21.26%	518,571	3,631,276	104,551	3,735,827	31.49%	1,176,412
2020	2,957,686	87,991	3,045,677	21.91%	667,220	4,912,239	87,991	5,000,230	18.40%	920,042
2021	3,712,897	116,638	3,829,535	16.64%	637,293	5,920,272	116,638	6,036,910	28.71%	1,733,197
2022	4,466,828	115,769	4,582,597	-18.71%	-857,615	7,770,107	115,769	7,885,876	-18.11%	-1,428,132
2023	3,724,982	116,000	3,840,982	10.65%	409,018	6,457,743	116,000	6,573,743	26.29%	1,728,237
2024	4,250,000		4,250,000			8,301,981		8,301,981		

If you have a 401(k) plan, do a comparison on how your 401(k) plan has done, compared to just investing in the S&P 500 index fund on your own. Do this now—don't wait until you're ready to retire. Go to: https://www .doctorace.com/resources/ and download the free Excel comparison sheet to see how your investments have done against the S&P 500 fund. Use your annual 5500, which is sent to the IRS each year to fill out this Excel sheet.

To obtain the 5500, go to: https://www.efast.dol.gov/5500search/ and put in your EIN number to get copies of past 5500s. Go to Part III, 7a to find the beginning-of-the-year balance and, next to that, the end-of-the-year balance. The ending balance will be the same for the beginning balance of the next year. Then go to part 8a (1,2,3) to put in the total contributions for that year. It is that simple. This will help you realize how much you have lost or gained in your retirement account by using the various advisers and mutual funds.

You can also use this Excel sheet to compare how well your financial adviser has done investing your money in your personal account. Compare your personal investment account to the S&P 500. If the results are poor, you need to transfer your portfolio into an account that you have control of and make your own investment decisions. If this is not possible as an employee in your 401(k), then just put in the employer's match, and place it into a low-cost index fund. If you are the employer, you may want to set up a self-directed 401(k) plan through Charles Schwab. Phone Schwab at 877-456-0777. https://www.youtube.com/watch?v=W7oVm3RJw_0

Warren Buffett has said that the late Jack Bogle has probably done more for the American investor than any man in the country. He is the father of the indexed mutual fund and, in *MarketWatch* said: "If you pay a hefty fee to an active manager, what happens to your potential return? Answer: Nothing good. A 2.5% fee over a typical investor's lifetime, an astounding 75% of compounding returns end up in the hands of the manager, not the investor." Bogle believes that actively managed funds are a big scam.

When you invest in loaded, actively managed mutual funds, you put up 100% of the capital and take 100% of the risk. If you make money, your fund manager takes up to 70% or more of the upside in fees. If you lose money, they still get paid. They are charging you 10 to 30 times what it would cost for you to buy a low-cost index fund that would match the market and beat 90% of the actively managed mutual funds.

Fees of only 1% per year can slash the value of your savings by 28% over the next 35 years, according to the Department of Labor. These are in addition to other fees in actively managed funds such as trading costs, taxes, and hidden fees.

Most individual investors put their money in mutual funds and rely upon money managers, financial advisers, and brokers who engage in hyperactive trading to try to beat the market by picking winners and timing. This is a losing strategy. More than 96% of investors would be better off consistently investing on their own in an S&P 500 index fund (SWPPX).

Expenses and fees are the enemy of the individual investor. You must understand that advisers, brokers, and mutual fund managers are well-meaning salespeople. If you invest $4,000 per month on your own in an index S&P 500 fund for 30 years at 7% return, you will have earned $3,781,475. With a 1% fee, your financial adviser will take 25% of your earnings over time. With a 2% fee, they will take 46% of your earnings; with a 3% fee, they will take 62% of your earnings; with a 4% fee, they will take 75% of your earnings. Your advisers will always get paid, even when you lose money in market downturns. See the chart below.

Advisory/Fund % fee	The money Advisory/Fund will take from you	% Return of your earnings
1%	$962,322	25%
2%	$1,725,989	46%
3%	$2,332,220	62%
4%	$2,820,600	75%

"Unfortunately, the vast majority of those who call themselves financial advisers neither charge a fair price nor give good advice. More than any other market I know, the market for financial advice is 'Let the buyer beware.'"— Jim Dahle, M.D.

Remember, the person who cares the most about your money is you. Learn to invest on your own, and stay away from financial advisers and brokers who work on commission.

"You must unlearn what you have learned."
—YODA

As Yoda taught in *Star Wars*, the first step is letting go of how you have been programmed in the past. Take charge and control of your own money and stop playing the bankers', advisers', and financial institutions' game. The new model described in this book will eliminate your money stress and bring peace back into your life.

Learn How to Invest Safely and Simply on Your Own

A verse from the Eagles song "Already Gone" says, "So often times it happens that we live our lives in chains, and we never even know we have the key." The key to your personal and financial independence is to get out of debt quickly and learn how to invest in the stock market safely on your own. This can be easily done risk free through paper trading without the help of a financial adviser and their outrageous management fees. Paper trading will be described below. It is like taking a college course in investing. Is your financial freedom worth this amount of time? In this book, you will be taught a specific game plan to help you reach your investment goals and become financially free.

Rule One Investing

I'm about to share with you an easy-to-learn, effective investment strategy. It is not that complicated, and once you learn it, you will need to spend only an hour a month working on your investment portfolio. This is much better than entrusting your funds to a financial adviser or fund manager who might end up taking 75% of the money you have earned. Yes, initially it requires some time and action, but what I'll guide you through is so straightforward that anyone, even those with no prior investment experience or aversion to math, can manage it. Using this approach, you could obtain an annual return of 15%, which would double the 7% average market return.

To make this happen for yourself, you need to understand the rules. Every successful investor, whether actively trading or a long-term investor, abides by Warren Buffet's two rules: rule #1—Don't lose money, and rule #2—Don't forget rule #1.

The embodiment of this philosophy can be found in the books written by Phil Town entitled: *Rule #1, Payback Time, and Invested*—all national bestsellers. In these books, he helps you find wonderful companies using technical tools to help you determine the true valuation of a company. This will help you purchase these companies at the best time and the best price. This will be discussed in this chapter. Check out his website at: https://www. ruleoneinvesting.com/

If you want to retire financially independent, you must learn to grow your retirement funds on your own. This will also give you the extra funds needed to enjoy your life before you eventually step away from the workforce.

Investing safely and predictably in the stock market is the fastest way to grow wealth through compound interest.

Albert Einstein once said:. "Compound interest is the eighth wonder of the world. He who understands it, earns it . . . he who doesn't, pays it." Here is a real-life example.

When I was at Command and General Staff College back in 1981, the post commander, Lieutenant General Howard Stone, spoke to the entire school one afternoon on finances. He told us to pay attention to where we spend our money, and to put 10% to 15% toward debt reduction and savings. The saved money should be put into an IRA. This will teach us the power of compound interest.

At that time, the maximum you could put in was $2,000, so I took $4,000 and funded my IRA for 1981 and 1982 with a broker at Edward Jones. He put me into a good loaded mutual fund that, fortunately, gave the same return as the S&P 500 index fund. That was the only time I ever invested in the market until the year 2000. General Stone wasn't around, so I never looked at or worried about that investment for 18 years.

In January 2000, I was shocked to see my $4,000 had grown to $105,000, an overall return of twenty-six times. This is when I began to understand the power of compound interest. At a 15% annual return, that $105,000 would have grown from 2000 to 2024 to more than $3.76 million. Remember that this was a one-time investment of only $4,000, which grew to $3.76 million over 42 years.

If that money had been invested in a Roth IRA with a 3% dividend yield, I would be getting more than $110,000 tax free that year. With more than a 10% dividend growth rate, my income could triple in 10 years. Just think how many millions of dollars I would have had if I had put in the maximum to my IRA account each year from 1982 and understood how to invest it safely on my own.

Many individuals get confused with investing and do not understand how easy it is to invest on their own through a company like Charles Schwab. That is why they are so vulnerable to dangerous investment schemes and high-fee advisers and brokers that will destroy any chance for them to have a comfortable retirement.

> *"The problem in America isn't so much what people don't know;*
> *the problem is what people think they know that just isn't so."*
> —WILL ROGERS

Everything you have been taught about money makes other people wealthy and keeps you poor. Learning to invest on your own and creating wealth is not complicated! The secret to becoming financially free is to make more money in your work and quickly pay off debt. During this time, you can learn how to trade in the stock market using risk-free paper trading as described below. Also learn how to maximize your personal investments in a tax-free environment.

These options are never offered to you by your financial advisers because no one makes money from them. What you are offered are risky stocks and mutual funds with low returns, high commissions, and advisory fees, along with the high anxiety associated with these products. The other supposedly safe type of investment are low-return bonds or treasuries that will never provide adequate passive income for your life.

How to Start

The idea of investing on your own and understanding stocks and the stock market can seem overwhelming. It is not that hard once you learn a simple and systematic approach to picking great companies and buying them when they are on sale. By learning to invest now, you will be able to create a constant source of increasing passive income for you and your family over your lifetime. This chapter gives you an insight and overview of the investing process.

You do not have to be a genius to invest when you understand Rule One. It was created for the ordinary person just like you. Many people think you must take high risk to get high rewards in investing. This is just the opposite of Rule One investing. Here you can get high returns of 15% with low risk and reach retirement and financial independence a lot sooner.

Over the long run, investing in the stock market produces the best returns of any investment. It is better than bonds, better than gold, and even better than real estate if you do it the right way. When you buy stocks, you benefit in two ways: from any increases in the price of shares and from any dividends that the company pays to you as an investor.

To learn how to invest in the stock market and get the best returns, you will need a great teacher. I am not that teacher. But I can introduce you to my mentor, Phil Town, the founder of Rule One Investing. He will help and coach you through this process. He believes that, with the proper one-on-one personal training, you could average more than 15% annual return on your investments in the stock market. I have found this to be true for me and get no compensation for sharing this information.

You will find much valuable information on his website, his books, and through his three-day virtual webinar. You are not going to learn how to best invest from this book or from any other book any more than you can learn to fly a plane by reading about flying in a book. You must go fly the plane and get the feel of it for real. To accelerate your learning experiences without making fateful mistakes, learn paper trading. This is taught in his hands-on Zoom course. Here you will learn a step-by-step approach on how to invest like Warren Buffett for only $97. These three days are your first step to financial freedom.

https://www.ruleoneinvesting.com/virtual-investing-workshop/.

This Zoom course is the best I have ever taken to learn how to invest on my own without risk through paper trading. It is personally taught by Phil Town himself along with his great instructors. In my small Zoom group of 8 students, we had 2 instructors to hand-hold us through each process and showed us how to find great companies and buy them at half price.

Also check out his website and his blogs on learning to invest, financial control, stock basics, investment news and tips, retirement planning, and personal development.

https://www.ruleoneinvesting.com/blog/stock-market-basics/become -investor/

https://www.ruleoneinvesting.com/blog/stock-market-basics/how-the-market -works/

https://www.ruleoneinvesting.com/blog/how-to-invest/value-investing/

You first need to set up an account in a brokerage house that has a great trading platform and the tools and indicators to help you understand when the best time is to get in or to get out of the market. I recommend Charles Schwab. I have no connection with Charles Schwab, other than I like and use their services. They have low or no fees for trading stocks, a user-friendly interface, easy-to-understand trading platform and incredible customer service.

It is an American multinational financial-services company. It offers banking, commercial banking, an electronic trading platform, and wealth-management advisory services to both retail and institutional clients. It has more than 360 branches, primarily in financial centers in the United States and the United Kingdom. It is the 13th-largest banking institution in the United States, with more than $6.6 trillion in client assets. It is one of the three largest asset managers in the world.

Charles Schwab is open 24 hours a day, 7 days a week, and has excellent representatives and brokers. Schwab has no dollar minimums to open an account. It has one of the lowest expense ratios for the S&P 500 funds. When you purchase stocks and index ETFs (exchange-traded funds), there are no trading fees or commissions..

While Schwab was designed to sell stocks and provide stock investors with the most current research and other useful information, they offer everything that any big bank would offer, including checking and savings accounts.

All representatives and Schwab brokers are salaried; they do not work on commission, so their advice focuses on your best interests. Schwab has agents located in most large cities. These local Schwab brokers can help you open an account, but it may be easier to go online and have an account set up within 30 minutes. You can call their online representative (800-435-4000) to help you through this process. Set up your Charles Schwab account:

https://www.schwab.com/client-home

Once you set up an account, you'll then need to "fund" your Charles Schwab cash account (not margin account) by linking it to your personal bank accounts. Call up a Schwab representative to help you create this link. Within a day, you will be able to transfer money from your own bank account into your Schwab investment account. Once it is set up, then transfer the amount of money you plan to invest. You can also set up an automatic transfer each month if you would like. Initially, there is no money needed to open an account.

Another option is to just send a check to Schwab. Check with a representative to verify the correct address to send the check and write your name and account number on the check. After your brokerage account is set up, download the Charles Schwab app onto your phone.

They recently acquired Ameritrade and their trading platform, called *thinkorswim*. This is one of the best platforms to help you practice trading in the stock market without risk, using paper trades. Not only is it a great platform for determining when to buy in and get out of stocks but also for those who are interested in option trading. Ask your Schwab representative how to download and use *thinkorswim*. Check out the YouTube videos on how to use *thinkorswim*. This is your golden ticket to becoming a successful investor.

https://www.youtube.com/watch?v=W5gJ5-p-8O8&list=PL5F91D714FC3C
DE21&index=1

Understanding Rule One Investing

This system is not that hard to learn. My 12-year-old grandson is using what he learned in this course to invest in his Roth IRA. This is how you teach and create generational wealth. Of the many different investing strategies that a modern-day investor may choose, value investing is the best. It is also the foundation of the Rule One investing strategy. Once you learn this system, you will need to spend only 15 minutes a week possibly doing option trading and following the statistics of the 6 to 15 companies you own or want to own.

Warren Buffett recommends that investors concentrate their investments in a limited number of well-known, high-quality businesses. During a talk at Georgetown University on Sept. 19, 2013, Buffett described the punch-card strategy approach as follows: *"You have an opinion on only a few things. In fact, I've told students that, if, when they got out of school, they should get a punch card with 20 punches on it, and that's all the investment decisions they got to make in their entire life; they would get very rich because they would think very hard about each one."*

Quite simply, invest as if you had only 20 investing possibilities in your lifetime. For the punch-card approach to work, you find and research wonderful companies that you can purchase at half price. Then invest for the long run. It prevents investors from succumbing to the urge to trade excessively and concentrate on the best companies, resulting in long-term rewards.

Here are the steps to Rule One investing. First, we must find a wonderful company. To help us, we use the Rule One toolbox scanner to create a watch list of wonderful companies and the price you are willing to pay. These are the businesses you want to own and that you will buy if the price is right. Your Watch List won't be long. Over time, you may have only 6 to 15 companies that you own. A portfolio of 6 to 15 high-quality income stocks spread out reasonably over different sectors provides a compelling balance between the benefits of diversification and of concentration. One of the best places to find great companies is through the Rule One toolbox search section.

The toolbox will help us determine the true intrinsic retail value of the company. Next, we calculate the margin-of-safety price of these companies. This is usually 50% of the intrinsic retail value of the company. When the price drops to our margin-of-safety price, which is half of the retail value price, we buy the company. If the price continues to drop, then we will buy more shares as long as it still remains a wonderful company. When the company grows over time to exceed 20% of the intrinsic retail value, we may want to sell the company. We use this money to buy other undervalued companies or to buy the same company when it is on sale for half price. We continue to do this until we are rich.

Our goal is to have 6 to 15 wonderful companies that we own. While we wait for the margin-of-safety price, we can do option trading. The Rule One Zoom course will teach you how to do option trading with very little risk, with a potential annual return of 20%. This takes only about 15 minutes per week to either see if the company is ready to buy or to put in your option trades.

Value investing is a strategy focusing on buying companies with a low price-to-earnings multiple. Ben Graham, Warren Buffett's mentor, is the father of value investing and wrote the bible of value investing; " Security Analysis" in 1934. This book is still in print today.

He called this "value" investing because, ideally, each investment had more value than was paid in the price. In essence, the idea is to get $10 of value for a $5 price.

By the time Warren Buffett started investing money, though, the economy had changed, and finding deeply undervalued companies was not as easy as it had been in Graham's time. To adapt, Buffett adjusted the theory somewhat, choosing to focus on finding companies that were not only undervalued but were also wonderful businesses with a highly predictable future. Buffett also recommends that you buy only companies that you understand. He calls this your "circle of competence."

Rule One investing dictates that the best way to make large returns on your investments is to find a few intrinsically wonderful companies run by good people and priced much lower than their actual value. A business that hits all these marks constitutes a Rule One company.

Finding Wonderful Companies

Wonderful companies have products that are universal, they have honest management, can raise prices during inflationary times, they maintain large profit margins, have little or no debt, and make the world a better place.

Use the 4-Ms and the Rule One Toolbox to Find Great Companies

First you must ensure that the companies you are investing in are high-quality enough to retain their value throughout the time you are holding them. I like to evaluate whether a business is a wonderful company with what I call the 4-Ms of Investing: Meaning, Management, Moat, and Margin of Safety. Of the four, the margin of safety does not tell you if it is a good company, but it does help you buy these wonderful companies at half price.

Meaning—You must understand the meaning of the business. How does this industry work, who are the competitors, and how do they compete? And how does this business fit your personal values? Does it have meaning to you personally? This is important because if it has meaning to you, you'll better understand what it does and how it works. You'll be more likely to do the research necessary to understand all elements of the business that affect its value.

Management—The company needs to have management that is talented and has integrity. Perform a background check on the leaders in charge of guiding the company, paying close attention to their honesty, transparency, and success of their prior positions to determine if they are good, solid leaders that will take the company in the right direction. And, super critical, do they allocate capital well?

Moat—The company should have a moat. A moat is something intrinsic to business, making it very difficult for competitors to compete. If a company has patented technology, a network of users, control over the market, an impenetrable brand, or a product or service customers would never switch from, it has a moat. Commodity companies rarely have a moat and are not usually on our watch list.

Margin of Safety—To guarantee good returns, you must buy a company at a price that gives you a margin of safety. For Rule One investors, 50% off the intrinsic value (retail price) is the margin of safety to look for. This provides a buffer that makes it possible to still experience gains even if problems arise. This is the final M, but arguably the most important.

These 4-Ms separate Rule One investing from value investing. Both dictate that you must buy a company at a good price, but Rule One strategy requires a much deeper understanding of the business. We reduce risk with knowledge. That's the bottom line.

Determine the Companies' Intrinsic Value

At its core, a Rule One stock is a company that is priced at half of its intrinsic value (fair market value/retail price). The problem is knowing what is the true intrinsic value. This term is thrown around a lot regarding value investing. The key to your investing success is to buy companies at the margin-of-safety price, which is half of the intrinsic value price. One of the best ways of finding this is to use the Rule One toolbox.

Phil Town, in his books and in his courses, discusses three ways of determining the intrinsic value of a company. These are called the Margin of Safety, Payback Tome, and 10 Cap. There are different valuation methods for companies, depending on where the company is in its life cycle. Here are the three methodologies.

Margin of Safety involves buying a stock at a price significantly below its intrinsic value. It provides a buffer against errors in estimation and unforeseen adverse events. This method is best used for younger companies who are in higher growth and are putting a lot of their money back into growing the business. A great example of a company where this valuation method would be used is Netflix.

Payback time refers to the estimated time it takes for an investor to recoup their initial investment through the company's future free-cash flows. Investors using the payback-time method want to identify stocks where the expected free-cash flows will allow them to recover their investment within a reasonable time fare. Paypal is an example of a company where we might use this method.

The 10 Cap (capitalization rate) valuation method is a favorite among some investors because it is the easiest to do, and it doesn't depend on coming up with some arbitrary growth rate for the next 10 years which is just unknowable. All I have to know is: "Will this company be bigger and better in 10 years? This method is great for up-and-coming companies, like Sprouts Farmers Market. We can ask simple questions like: Will there be more stores in 10 years? If the answer is "Yes," we take the annual earnings, multiply by 10 and achieve the valuation.

These calculations require tools and practice to fully know and understand which methodology to use, how to do the calculations and attach an accurate intrinsic value. This is why they teach this in their three-day virtual Zoom workshops. They are automatically calculated in the toolbox under "research valuation calculator." These are used only as guidelines because you need to do your own research on each of these companies. They also have a graph that shows you the buy price, 20% above the buy price, the sticker price and 20% above the sticker price. See below these evaluations on Ulta Beauty Inc (ULTA).

Then calculate the sticker price is $680.62 and the buy price at $340.31. The current price is $378 which is very close to the buy price. As you can see from the toolbox ULTA has the highest Rule One score of 100, indicating it is a wonderful company.

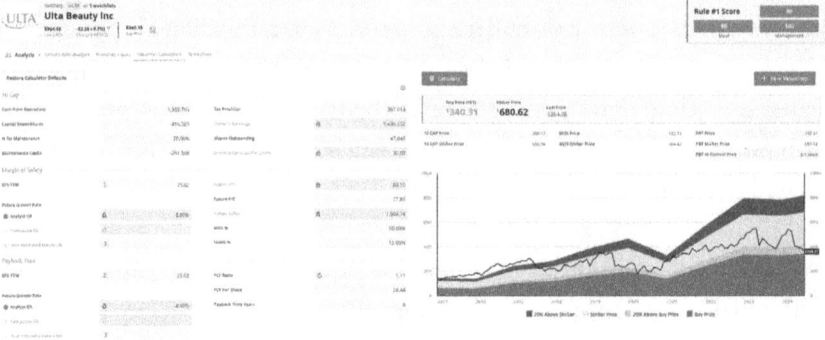

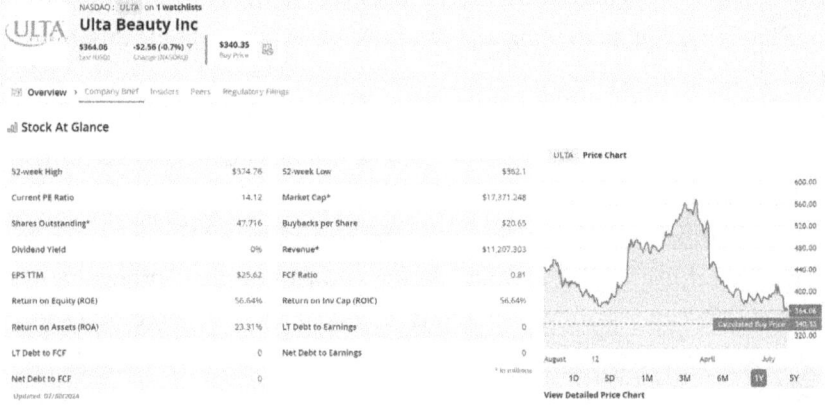

The reason we do all three is to verify that they are telling the same story! It's like a system of checks and balances to make sure we fully understand the business and are able to make an investment that will deliver maximum returns for years to come.

How do you decide when to use these things? Initially, run all three. A lot of companies, particularly with growth rates of 15% to 20%, have valuations very similar. Just add them up, divide by three, and take the average.

When the growth rates are low, 5% to 8% growth with a low PE ratio, your margin-of-safety valuation is going to be a lot lower than the 10 cap and the payback time. In that case, we don't just add them all together but use the two that are very similar. Occasionally all three of them are all over the map; then consider that a red flag, and look for another company.

Another method that is very helpful in determining if the stock is undervalued is to look at the price of the stock over its 52-week range. Focus on stocks that are close to their 52-week low point. Using ULTA as an example, above, you can see that the stock lies very close to its 52-week low.

52 Week Range

368.02   ●▬▬▬▬▬▬▬▬▬▬▬▬▬   574.76

Buying stocks when they are undervalued is one of the most important criteria in stock selection. Our goal is to buy wonderful companies at half the sticker price when they are on sale. Wait until these companies' price ranges are at the lower end of their 52-week low/high range.

Many investors look for companies that are cheap. Rule One investor knows that it is better to buy a wonderful business at a fair price than a fair business at a wonderful price. Rule One investors require a deep understanding of the companies before they buy. They must know the business well enough and understand that it's wonderful. This mindset is an important step in learning value investing. While it may not appear all that complex, buying $10 bills for $5 can be an emotional challenge, but with the right mindset, most can master it.

Warren Buffett has said that emotions are the enemy of a rational investor. The biggest problem with young investors is overconfidence in believing that they know more than they know. This is called conformational bias, where you can no longer see anything negative about the company. All great investors look at inversion. Before they make a decision to buy a company, they look at all the things that can go wrong or what is bad with the company.

Fear is your friend. Buffett said that the secret to great investing results is to buy when there is **Fear! Fear** is what makes the market price of a wonderful business fall substantially lower than its intrinsic value.

Focus on the Long Term. Buy businesses at the right time, and know that the right time will present itself if you're patient. Everyday stock-market volatility and events such as recessions, market crashes, negative publicity, among others, create opportunities for value investors to jump in and buy when the price drops. We want to see the market go down so that we can buy great companies at a significant discount.

An example of such an event was the E coli scare with Chipotle Mexican Grill (CMG) in 2015, when the stock dropped from $700.00 a share down to $250 a share in 2018. This was a strong, well-run company that rebounded from a low of $250 a share to $3280 a share on Tuesday, June 25, 2024. It has since had a 50 to 1 stock split as of June 26 to the price of $66 post-stock split.

Finding underpriced wonderful companies does not happen every day. Charlie Munger said we don't make money when we buy, and we don't make money when we sell; **we make money when we wait.** While we wait for wonderful companies to go on sale, we spend very little time on investing while enjoying the fun parts of life. During our free time, we do our research to create a watch list of wonderful companies that we want to buy. For those investors who want to try to maximize their investment assets, they can learn how to trade options safely.

In the 1960s, when Warren Buffett had only a small amount of money to invest, he was able to get annual returns of up to 50% by finding smaller undervalued growth companies with great potential. Over the past 10 years, Buffet's returns have only matched the S&P 500 because of his size and inability to move in and out of the market quickly. Small individual investors like ourselves have a great advantage over large institutional investors. We have the advantage of finding smaller undervalued wonderful companies with great potential that are not on the radar of large investors. Use the toolbox scanner to help find these companies.

Learn to invest with great teachers. Once you have learned, become an independent thinker, and make your own purchase decisions. Try not to rely on other people to give you your recommendations.

Research Sources and Websites

Today we have many great Internet resources to quickly look for and research wonderful companies. The best one I have found is the Rule One toolbox https://www.ruleonetoolbox.com/login. You can sign up for a 14-day free trial. You will also get three months free when you take the $97.00 three-day Zoom video workshop. The monthly cost is about $30.

Here, you can get information that is hard to get anywhere else. Through their stock scanner, you can filter stocks based on specific parameters. Some of these parameters may be a market cap greater than $300 million, long-term debt less than two years of earnings, return on investment capital (ROIC) of 15% or greater, and a Rule One safety score of 85% or greater. You may want to eliminate from your search all companies that are biotech or pharmaceutical, those that are pure technology, those that are banks or insurance companies, and any companies from China. These are just examples.

You can search for the important numbers of great companies using the Rule One criteria for calculating growth rates, the moat and management numbers, and pricing and valuations. It has links to the company's annual reports and 10K's plus a list of what companies the investment gurus are buying or selling. It even color-codes the results so you can easily see which companies to look at and which companies you should avoid. You will learn how to use this toolbox when you take the Rule One virtual three-day course and receive a three-month subscription to the toolbox for free. https://www.youtube.com/watch?v=wmuPCLOo4U8&t=292s

The best resource for investment terminology is https://www.investopedia.com/. Below are the best free investment-research websites that I use to do my research. They also have good stock screeners. You can go on YouTube to see how they work. There are upgrades you can purchase for more in-depth research.

Charles Schwab (free)—https://client.schwab.com/app/research/#/tools/stocks

Seeking Alpha (free)—https://seekingalpha.com/

Yahoo finance (free)—https://finance.yahoo.com/

There are also three YouTube sites that I use in my research. They are:

New money—https://www.youtube.com/@NewMoneyYouTube/videos

Investor center—https://www.youtube.com/@InvestorCenter/videos

Rule 1 investing—https://www.youtube.com/@PhilTownRule1Investing

Red Flags—In chapter 5 of Phil Town's *Payback Time*, he lists six red flags that you need to watch out for when selecting a company. The **first** is that it has no meaning to you. If you're not an expert in an industry, you don't have any business owning a company in that industry. **Second**, it has no moat. If there is no durable competitive advantage, don't even consider it. Without a moat, a business has to compete on price. **Third**, the CEO is a poor leader without vision or strong values.

Fourth, the company cannot pay off its debt within three years. To check this, divide the total long-term debt by current earnings. Ideally, we would like to see no debt. **Fifth**, the company has powerful trade unions that can destroy its competitive edge. **Sixth**, be careful of technology companies, as their moat can disappear overnight with new technology.

Paper Trading

In the virtual course, you will learn how to set up a *thinkorswim* trading platform and use it to practice with paper money (you get $100,000 in Monopoly-like play money). This will help you overcome the fear of investing and the possibility of losing money while you learn how to invest safely. Once you open a trading account with Charles Schwab, call them; let them help you download the *thinkorswim* platform and show you how to make a paper trade. Set up your *thinkorswim* platform indicators following the YouTube link below:

https://www.youtube.com/watch?v=dr9r9AQL1p0

To paper-trade, you start by searching for a business that's wonderful and available at an attractive price. Use the toolbox to help you focus your search. Do the 4-M analysis on businesses until you find one that works for you. In your notebook, write down the name of the business and the symbol, the Sticker Price, and the MOS Price. Charles Schwab will usually start you out with $100,000 of fake money to practice with. Review the indicators for the businesses you want to buy, and when you have three indicators that say "Get in," buy the business on paper.

Open a Charles Schwab account for your children, and set up their own *thinkorswim* platform. Teach them to invest in the stock market without fear and enjoy the process of buying and selling stocks using paper money on *thinkorswim*. This will be better than any of the video games they're playing now.

Think or Swim Indicators, FACs, and Trend Lines

Stocks move up or down, not so much to events that are happening. Events can and do affect the decision of the institutional fund manager to buy or sell the stocks, but, in the end, the price of the stock goes up or down only because of increased or decreased institutional investing. Because the big guys are more than 80% of the market, it takes them 6 to 12 weeks to get totally in or out of a company. For small investors like us, it takes us only about 10 seconds to do the same.

Since January 2014, Warren Buffett's Berkshire Hathaway and the S&P 500 has had the same annualized rate of return, including reinvestment of dividends of 12%. The reason Buffett is not getting the high returns as he did in the past is because he is too big and cannot move in and out of the market as quickly as we can. This allows us to get greater returns than the S&P 500.

Being small gives us a great advantage over these large institutional investors. To help us identify when the big boys are getting in and out, we use tools known as technical indicators. There are three indicators that are very helpful, and when all of them line up saying "buy," it's time to get in. When all three are saying "sell," it's time to get out. Simple.

Once you have identified a wonderful business that passes all 4-Ms and can buy it at 50% margin of safety, these indicators help you have the courage to invest in those great companies. These indicators are fantastic at keeping you from losing money if you are buying businesses at prices below their value (the sticker price). The only way to make money with certainty in any kind of investment is to buy it well below its value. Doing that will make you very rich.

The best source are the Charles Schwab 3 indicators found on their trading platform called *thinkorswim*. Once you've downloaded the platform, use the following YouTube link to set up these indicators correctly. https://www.youtube.com/watch?v=dr9r9AQL1p0. These indicators are described in more detail in chapter 12 in Phil Town's book; Rule #1: The Simple Strategy for Getting Rich—in Only 15 Minutes a Week!

The first indicator is called a moving average. This tool tracks the average price of a stock during a specific time period. Moving averages are simply closing prices over a defined number of days divided by that number of days. There are a lot of technical traders out there who trigger their buying and selling with a moving average. The moving average smooths out the peaks and valleys of daily price fluctuations and gives traders an easy view of the price trend.

Technical traders (which we are not) don't even think about what a business is worth. All they want to know is whether it's going to move up or down based on these or similar indicators. Technical traders make their buying and selling decisions based solely on price and do not undergo an analysis of the fundamentals of the company. They don't care about anything else except price movements. When the price line crosses above the moving average line, they buy. When the price line crosses below the moving average line, they sell.

The second indicator is the MACD—Moving Average Convergence Divergence. Developed by an economist, Dr. Gerald Appel, the MACD is probably the most consistent indicator of significant trend changes in a stock, and it's certainly the most used technical indicator in the world. It looks at several price average changes over time, generally in the short term. It shows us when momentum pressure is getting stronger either upward or downward. Since most of the money in the market is institutional, the MACD shows us when the big guys are sneaking in or sneaking out. The MACD is the combination of two moving averages—a fast one and a slow one—and how they interact.

The third indicator is the slow stochastic, developed by Dr. George C. Lane. This is a momentum tool that tracks the overbuying and overselling of a stock. The Stochastic looks at the high price and the low price of a stock over a 14-trading-days period. When the price goes below the 20th percentile, the stock is getting oversold—too many sellers and not enough buyers.

When it moves up through the 20th percentile, it often means the big guys are starting to seriously buy and that the price is likely to go up. When the price moves well above the 80th percentile, the stock is going into an overbought condition— too many buyers and not enough sellers. As it drops below the 80th percentile, it indicates the big guys were seriously taking profits, and the price is likely to drop.

Here is an example of using *thinkorswim* and the three indicators we have discussed set for monthly charting, using T Rowe Price as our example from July 2019 until February 2024. In March 2019, you were able to see the three arrows in the monthly chart going up and get in at $112. In December 2021, you saw the three arrows going down and you would have gotten out at \$200. We then wait for the three arrows to go up in May 2023 and buy in at \$108. In March 2019 the stochastic had no green arrow, but the line was moving upward, which qualifies as a green arrow.

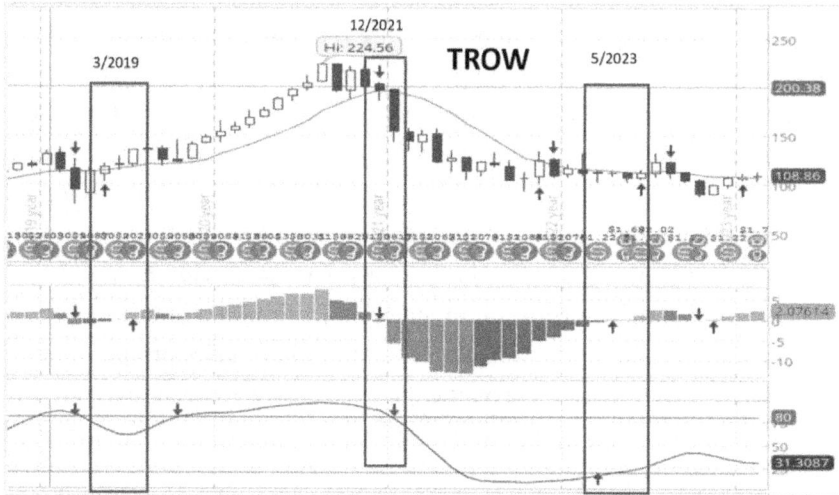

These indicators do help us in our buying decisions, but we first need to do our research to determine if this is a wonderful company to buy. Then focus on the 4-Ms and the true intrinsic value of the company, and buy it at half price. If we ignore the 4-Ms and accidentally buy businesses that are priced above their value, the prices of those businesses will eventually correct themselves downward toward the Sticker Price, and we lose money.

These indicators are very helpful when we're trying to buy businesses below their intrinsic value (the Sticker Price). The only way to make money with certainty in any kind of investment is to buy it well below its intrinsic value.

Floors and Ceilings (FACs)

The Floors and Ceilings is a strategy for timing stock purchases based on the recurring patterns in a stock's price movement, utilizing psychological cues known as Floors and Ceilings (FACs). FACs play a crucial role in optimizing the timing of stockpiling, particularly when aiming for substantial discounts to the MOS (Margin of Safety) Price.

As value investors, we wait to buy a great company when it is at or below 50% of its sticker price, which is called "Margin of Safety." At that time, we will stockpile. This is a term used to indicate initially putting a portion of our total capital we want to invest in the business, such as 25%. We then take advantage of the floors and ceilings lines to add another 25% or 50% as the stock drops lower and hits the floor.

FACs are rooted in the understanding that significant market players, such as fund managers controlling substantial sums in the market, tend to fixate on specific price targets. Although psychological in nature, FACs hold tangible significance. For instance, if a fund manager decides to buy a stock at $70 based on historical bounces at that price, it becomes a psychological floor in the price, akin to a solid foundation.

Observing any stock-price chart reveals that prices seldom ascend continuously; periodic reversals are inherent, even in bullish markets. These pullbacks are influenced by the emotions and psyche of investors, particularly the influential Big Guys. These market players may get apprehensive or overly optimistic, prompting them to initiate selling when this perceives a potential peak in the stock's price.

This time-consuming process of exiting positions requires anticipation of a mass exit, leading to selling actions. While selling safeguards against overstaying in the market, it also allows fund managers to realize profits. If the price stops declining after selling begins, fund managers might re-enter the market, starting another upward trajectory. This FACs stockpiling method labels a recurring price level a "Floor," signifying a point where a falling price tends to halt its descent. A Floor is identified when the price consistently rebounds off a specific level without breaking downward; the frequency of these bounces determines the strength of the Floor. Conversely, when the price ceases its ascent and either descends or stabilizes, the FAC method designates this recurring level as a "Ceiling," implying a barrier that the price struggles to surpass.

Notably, when a price finally reaches a Ceiling and moves upward, the former Ceiling often transforms into a new Floor. Stock prices exhibit a somewhat consistent pattern of movement between Floors and Ceilings before breaking through or possibly retracing to test the previous Ceiling as a new Floor.

On a price chart depicting a business's stock-price evolution, Floors and Ceilings are visualized as horizontal lines representing points where the price halts and reverses direction, shaped by recurrent reversals at specific price levels.

An additional element to consider is the Trend lines, depicted diagonally on the chart; these serve as imaginary boundaries that form a Resistance at the top and a Support at the bottom. Trend lines are imaginary diagonal lines that form over a long time. Floor and Ceiling lines are imaginary horizontal lines that form over a short time.

While distinct from Floors and Ceilings, Trend lines are used similarly to predict potential price reversals, offering an additional layer of analysis for strategic decision-making. You can draw these Floor and Ceiling lines as well as Trend lines using the drawing tools on your *thinkorswim* platform, as you see below.

Fibonacci Retracements help us see Floors and Ceilings (FACs) that may not be obvious at first glance. You can create Fibonacci retracements in *thinkorswim* by drawing lines between the high and low time. Generally, use a six-to-nine-month time frame day chart, and try to look for the best fit. See example below.

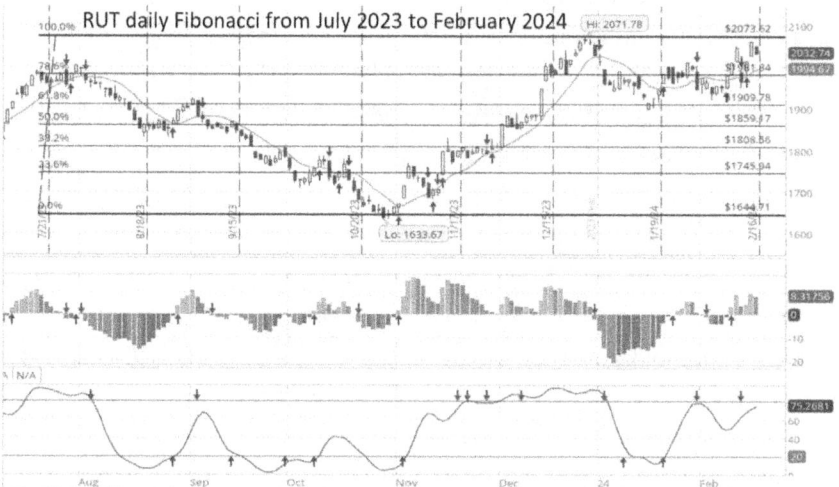

To learn more, read chapter 6 in Phil Town's *Payback Time* You will learn how to use these indicators during the three-day Rule One virtual workshop.

Three points to remember: 1. The more often the stock price bounces off the Floor or Ceiling, the stronger the Floor or Ceiling becomes. 2. To determine how far the price will climb from the new Floor to reach the next Ceiling, look at the distance between the last Floor and the last Ceiling. 3. A price move of more than 3 percent above the Ceiling or below the Floor, accompanied by 150 percent of the average daily volume of shares traded, is a significant sign of a breakout that will last.

Floors and Ceilings (FACs) are predictable patterns in the price charts that show you the appropriate time to buy and sell. You can stockpile any time the price is below the MOS/Payback Time price, but buying on the FACs will help you buy at the best possible price. To maximize your long-term investment returns, buy near the Floor price. Be patient!

Understanding Dividends

In today's investment landscape, there is a growing interest in acquiring stocks that offer dividends. It's appealing to possess ownership in a business and receive regular payments, akin to holding a treasury bill. Some individuals even consider dividends as the primary incentive for owning shares in a public company, as it represents tangible cash returns from the business itself. Dividends are disbursed by public enterprises for two distinct reasons, with only one being a sound rationale. I do not recommend the dividend reinvestment program (DRIP) because your dividends may be reinvested when the price of the stock is high. Use the cash dividends to live on, for option trading, or to purchase stocks that are undervalued.

The favorable reason is when a business accumulates more cash than it requires. A prudent CEO recognizes that this surplus belongs to the shareholders. The only justification for retaining it is if the CEO can utilize the funds to expand the business at a rate that justifies retaining the money. This growth rate is commonly known as Return on Equity (ROE), a critical metric. An effective CEO evaluates his team's performance, in part, based on how well they deploy owner capital. Indeed, overseeing the allocation of owner capital is arguably the CEO's most crucial responsibility. Returning the excess capital to shareholders becomes a legitimate option when the CEO cannot identify better investment opportunities.

The second reason is less commendable: some businesses allocate a portion of their earnings as a dividend to create the illusion of stability. This practice is influenced by Mr. Market, who prefers the appearance of steadiness over genuine stability. If earnings fluctuate, so does the dividend amount, causing unease for Mr. Market. He prefers a consistent dividend, resembling cash flow from a bond, and if this is achieved, he assigns a higher value to it. CEOs, responding to Mr. Market's preference, may establish an unwavering dividend quarter after quarter. This reliability attracts investors, especially retirees who mistakenly associate a consistent dividend with a stable business and therefore low risk. These investors will not want to sell the stock even if it's going down because this will cause them to miss out on their quarterly dividend payments.

Dividends make sense when a business has no superior alternatives for deploying your funds. For retirees relying on dividend income for their living expenses, investing in a robust business with consistent dividends is prudent, provided that these dividends stem from genuine, free cash flow. To ascertain whether dividends are derived from sources other than cash flow, a crucial step is to examine the Cash Flow Statement of the business.

When you're trying to select the best dividend companies to buy, many experts recommend that you focus on those companies that have continually increased their dividends every year for a long period of time. These are called dividend aristocrats, and champions that have increased their dividends earn for more than 25 years. Those companies that have increased their dividends for more than 50 years are called dividend kings.

This is a starting point, but the most important focus in any investing is to buy those companies that give the highest total equity return over time. I focus more on companies that have high annual-dividend growth and beat the S&P 500 over the last 10 years. Only 11 of the 56 dividend kings and 29 of the 90 dividend aristocrats and champions have done this.

To better understand why, let's compare two dividend kings. Lowe's (LOW) has increased their dividends for 63 years with a dividend yield of 2.08%. Northwest Natural (NWN) has increased their dividends for the past 66 years and has a dividend yield of 5.12%. If you chose Northwest Natural because of the high dividend yield, you would be making a big mistake. The focus must always be on the dividend growth and overall equity growth of the company.

Over the past 14 years, Lowe's, with a dividend yield of only 2.08% had its share price grow from $28 a share to $221 (789% increase) in equity value. During the same time frame, Northwest Natural, with a dividend yield of 5.12% had its **share price decreased** from $44 per share to only $37.42 per share (15% decrease). Next let's look at annual dividend income. Lowe's (LOW) 100 shares of annual dividend income grew from $40 to $460 (1150% increase) compared to your 100 shares with Northwest Natural (NWN), where your dividend income grew only from $174 to $195 (11% increase).

I would rather own Lowe's, which pays only a 2.08% dividend with an average 10-year annual dividend-growth rate of 19.8%, compared to NWN, which has a 5.12% dividend with an average 10-year dividend-growth rate of only 0.6%. Also, the Lowe's shares you bought 20 years ago are now paying a dividend return of 17% annually based on their original cost basis.

In 1988 Warren Buffett bought 23 million shares of Coca-Cola at a price of $2.73. With today's annual dividend rate of $1.94 per share, he gets an annual dividend return of 71% on the original shares bought. This year he will receive $776 million in dividends from Coca-Cola. Berkshire Hathaway does not pay dividends because Buffett feels he can better allocate the money for his investors. He still appreciates the power of dividend income and in 2024 will earn $6 billion in dividends from his investments.

This demonstrates the importance of focusing our purchases on companies with both high total equity growth and high dividend-growth rate. This leads to ever-increasing personal dividend income over time. In strong dividend-growth companies, the dividends income you receive continues to grow each year, even if the price of the stock drops. Over time, the price of these wonderful companies will rebound as your dividend income increases every year. Warren Buffett said, "Time is the friend of a wonderful company and the enemy of the mediocre."

Many wonderful companies increase their dividends each year. This increased income gives comfort to those who live off their dividends, especially during negative times in the market. Texas Instruments (TXN) is an example of a wonderful company that demonstrates both incredible dividend growth and equity growth. In 2024, Texas Instruments is now paying a dividend income return of 34.7% on the original cost basis shares bought in 2009. Over the past 14 years, their dividends have grown from $45 per 100 shares to $520 in 2024. This is 11.5 times increase in the dividends received over those years. In addition, a $100,000 investment in Texas Instruments in 2009 would have grown to more than $1.33 million in 2024.

Many retirees live on their dividends and unknowingly try to buy companies that have a high dividend yield without realizing that, over time, the value of their investment is continually decreasing. Do not be fooled by high dividend yields, as many companies will increase their dividend yield each year to lull shareholders into a false sense of security. This is why novice investors continue to hold the stock even as it continues to drop in value or the company goes bankrupt.

General Motors (GM) consistently paid dividends for many years even though they borrowed money to do so. In 2009 during the financial crisis, they filed for bankruptcy; all common stock of the old GM Corporation became worthless, and investors lost all their money.

Always evaluate the strength and growth of the company before you buy. Once you own a company, check on the vital statistics of that company monthly. Sell these companies when the key indicators such as return on investment capital (ROIC) decrease, making the company no longer wonderful. Stay away from any company that has a payout ratio above 60%. The 5- and 10-year annual growth of the company needs to be better than the S&P 500 as a guideline before you buy any dividend-paying companies.

To determine the stock's annual equity yield, including reinvestments of dividends, go to https://dqydj.com/stock-return-calculator/. To determine equity growth, dividend growth, and dividend yield, go to: https://seekingalpha.com/.

The dividend yield is a stock's annual dividend payment as a percentage of the stock price per share. Most dividend investors look for a yield somewhere between 2.5% and 6%. But the best total overall return comes from companies that have a lower-than 2.5% dividend yield. Over time, you will be getting a higher dividend return in these high dividend-growth companies.

In the example below, United Health (UNH) has a 1.48% dividend today. But the shares you bought 10 years before are now paying a dividend return of 10.2% based on the price of the stock then. The shares of United Health (UNH) that you bought 20 years ago are paying you 23.8% today based on your original share price. As they increased their yearly dividend, this return usually gets better and better over time.

You will notice in the chart below that the stock total return and dividend reinvestment came from those companies with lower dividend yields but had the highest 10-year average dividend-growth rates. Compare these companies with those on the bottom that have high dividend yield and low dividend-growth rates. The average annual return, including dividend reinvestment on these high-dividend-yield companies (IBM, WBA, KO and JNJ), have a significantly lower return than the lower-dividend-yield companies over the past 10 years.

Let's now look at Broadcom, ticker symbol AVGO. Its dividend yield was only 1.68% but a 10-year average dividend-growth rate of 39% and a whopping annual 10-year return of 39.5%. Over the past 10 years, a onetime **initial $10,000 investment grew to more than $272,000.** Compare this to Walgreen Boots Alliance (WBA), which had a 9.09% yield, and your initial investment of $10,000 declined to only $2,000 during that 10-year time frame, with dividends automatically reinvested. Over the same 10 years, $10,000 placed in the S&P 500 grew 3 times to $31,000.

It is important to keep high-returning companies on your watch list and take advantage of them when they become undervalued. You must wait for an event, such as we saw in March 2020, when the S&P 500 dropped 37%. This was a great time to buy these companies. Another event occurred in March 2009. Many great companies, such as Texas Instruments (TXN) and United Health (UNH) saw prices drop more than half. Texas Instruments dropped to $14.00 a share but grew to more than $200 a share by 2024. United Health Group went from $16.00 a share in 2009 to $600 a share by 2024. **Remember, "past performance is no guarantee of future results"!**

You will also note that most of the selected dividend-growth companies in the chart have a higher average annual return than the S&P 500 or even Warren Buffett's Berkshire Hathaway company.

Dividend Example: 3 September 2024

Ticker Symbol	Company	Sector	Cur Price	2014 Dividend	Dividend Yield	10Y ADGR	Cost basis Dividend yield in 10 years	Cost basis Dividend yield in 20 years	Annual total %return 2014 to 2024	$10k Return 2014 to 2024	SA 10 yr Total Return	P/E <20	Rule 1 Safety score
AVGO	Broadcom	IT	163	$2.10	1.29%	39.0%	9.7%	131.0%	37.2%	236	1753%	34	89
MSFT	Microsoft	IT	417	$3.00	0.72%	12.7%	8.1%	13.0%	26.4%	102	809%	32	98
AAPL	Apple Inc	IT	229	$1.00	0.44%	25.0%	5.0%	192.0%	26.0%	100	826%	34	89
COST	Costco	CS	892	$4.64	0.52%	12.8%	4.0%	15.5%	24.4%	87	693%	56	90
UNH	United Health	HC	590	$8.40	1.42%	25.6%	10.2%	23.5%	23.0%	78	573%	21	88
LOW	Lowe's	CD	249	$4.60	1.85%	18.9%	8.8%	17.0%	19.0%	57	359%	21	52
TXN	Texas Instruments	IT	214	$5.20	2.43%	22.4%	11.0%	21.0%	19.1%	57	341%	40	55
SHW	Sherwin-Williams	M	369	$2.86	0.78%	14.4%	4.8%	22.0%	18.6%	55	407%	32	64
HD	Home Depot	CD	369	$9.00	2.44%	20.3%	11.2%	25.0%	18.2%	53	302%	25	74
WSM	Williams Sonoma	CD	134	$2.28	1.70%	14.0%	7.8%	14.6%	18.0%	52	317%	17	97
BRK B	Berkshire Hathaway	ETF	476	$0.00	0.00%	NA	NA	NA	12.4%	32	244%	23	66
SPY	SPDR S&P500 ETF	ETF	563	$6.84	1.21%	7.4%	3.7%	6.0%	12.0%	31	180%	NA	NA
KO	Coca-Cola	CS	67	$1.94	2.90%	5.0%	4.9%	7.8%	8.4%	23	50%	25	53
JNJ	Johnson & Johnson	HC	166	$4.96	2.99%	6.0%	5.0%	9.0%	6.9%	21	45%	17	65
IBM	IBM	IT	202	$6.68	3.31%	5.8%	3.9%	7.9%	4.0%	15	-2%	17	35
WBA	Walgreen Boots	CS	9.25	$1.00	10.81%	1.5%	1.5%	3.0%	-15.0%	2	-85%	3	15

Chart categories:

Sectors: information technology, healthcare, consumer staples, materials, consumer discretionary, exchange traded funds.

Cur Price: this is the current stock price.

Dividend: annual dollar dividend per share per year.

Dividend Yield: the current annual yield as a percentage (dividend/price x 100).

10Y AGDR is the average annual dividend growth rate over the past 10 years. Dividend growth is the 2nd most important number in successful dividend investing over time. https://seekingalpha.com/symbol/AVGO/dividends/dividend-growth

Cost basis Dividend yield in 10 years: the current annual yield as a percentage (current dividend/2014 price= ? x 100 = %). (Example: in 2014 the price of Home Depot was $80 and the current annual dividend in 2024 is $9. You divide $9.00/$80.00 = .112 X 100 = 11.2% cost basis; you are now getting an 11.2% return today based on the price of the shares you bought 10 years before.

Cost basis dividend yield in 20 years: the current annual yield as a percentage (current dividend/2004 price= ? x 100 = %). (Example: in 2004 the price of Home Depot was $36 and the current annual dividend in 2024 is $9. You divide $9.00/$36.00 = .25 X 100 = 25% cost basis) you are now getting a 25% return today based on the price of the shares you bought 20 years before.

$10k Stock Total Return 2014 to 2024: the total return in dollars with a $10,000 initial investment after 10 years. This is the most important number in successful dividend investing over time. With AVGO, a $10,000 investment in 2014 would have grown to $286,000 in those 10 years. In 2014, a $10,000 investment with IBM would have grown to only $15,000 by 2024 in those 10 years. Stock Total Return and Dividend Reinvestment (DRIP) average for 10 years from June 2014 to June 2024. https://dqydj.com/stock-return-calculator/

SA 10 yr. Return: the total return on the stock after 10 years using the Seeking Alpha website.

PE<20: this is the price-to-earnings ratio (price/earnings). Ideally, we would like to see it below 20.

Rule One safety score: this comes from the Rule One toolbox that rates all stocks. The highest obtainable rating of 100 indicates a very strong and safe company, such as Microsoft, with a rating of 98, compared to a poor rating of 27 with IBM. The Rule One toolbox is a must for anyone who is involved in trading stocks.. https://www.ruleonetoolbox.com/login

Data found on July 2024—https://seekingalpha.com/; https://dqydj. com/stock-return-calculator/ and https://www.ruleonetoolbox.com/ below are examples using these websites for the chart above.

Seekingalpha.com charting is one of the best ways to compare any stock to the S&P 500. Check your portfolio stocks and funds in Seeking

Alpha to see how well you are doing. Below are examples of the 5 year and 10 year total returns of companies on the above chart.

AAPL: 338.82%
COST: 217.74%
LOW: 121.48%
SP500: 93.01%
IBM: 56.14%
JNJ: 29.21%
WBA: -81.93%
2024   08/30/2024

AAPL: 825.53%
COST: 692.63%
LOW: 359.25%
SP500: 181.33%
JNJ: 58.84%
IBM: 10.68%
WBA: -85.54%
2023   08/26/2024

https://dqydj.com/stock-return-calculator/ is used to determine the Stock Total Return between 2014 and 2024 in dollars with a $10,000 initial investment after 10 years. Here we compare Costco (COST) with Walgreen Boots Alliance (WBA)

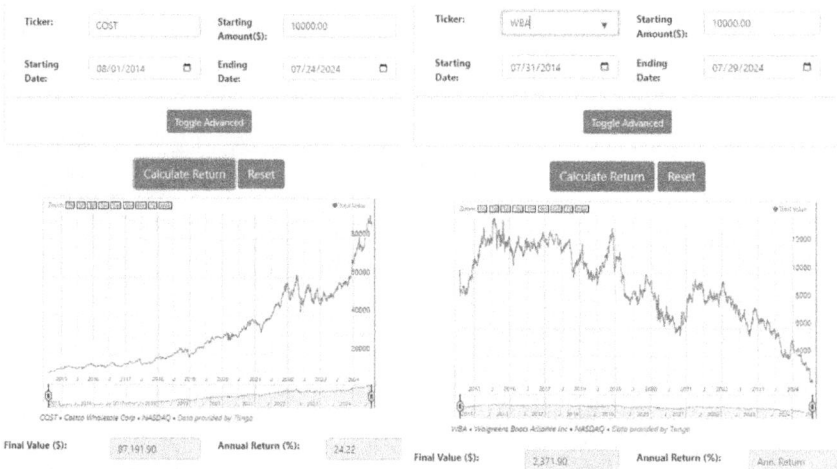

| Ticker: | COST | Starting Amount($): | 10000.00 |
| Starting Date: | 08/01/2014 | Ending Date: | 07/24/2024 |

Toggle Advanced

Calculate Return   Reset

COST • Costco Wholesale Corp • NASDAQ • Data provided by Tiingo

Final Value ($): 97,191.90   Annual Return (%): 24.22

| Ticker: | WBA | Starting Amount($): | 10000.00 |
| Starting Date: | 07/31/2014 | Ending Dates: | 07/29/2024 |

Toggle Advanced

Calculate Return   Reset

WBA • Walgreens Boots Alliance Inc • NASDAQ • Data provided by Tiingo

Final Value ($): 2,371.90   Annual Return (%): Ann. Return

https://www.ruleonetoolbox.com/ Costco (COST) with a moat score of 90 and a management score of 90 equaling and overall **Rule One score of 90** out of 100. **Walgreens Boots (WBA)** has a moat score of 13 and a management score of 15 equaling and overall **Rule One score of 14** out of 100.

NASDAQ : COST Costco Wholesale Corp

Rule One Scores

MOAT: Compound Growth Rate

	10 Years	7 Years	5 Years	3 Years	1 Year	Score
Book Value + Dividend + Buy Backs Growth	13.8%	13.9%	14.0%	11.0%	13.7%	100
Earnings Growth	11.9%	15.1%	15.0%	16.3%	7.7%	100
Total Revenue Growth	8.7%	10.7%	11.3%	13.2%	6.8%	96
Operating Cash Flow Growth	12.4%	18.9%	13.6%	7.9%	49.7%	98
Free Cash Flow Growth	17.0%	15.9%	15.2%	3.7%	92.7%	75
Rule One Moat Score						90

Management: Average Rate Of Return

	10 Years	7 Years	5 Years	3 Years	1 Year	Score
Return On Equity	23.6%	25.3%	25.6%	27.3%	25.1%	100
Return On Invested Capital	17.0%	18.3%	19.3%	21.0%	20.7%	100
Return On Assets	8.1%	8.6%	8.8%	9.2%	9.9%	50
Net Debt to Earnings					0.0 Years	100
Net Debt to Free Cash Flow					0.0 Years	100
Rule One Management Score						90

NASDAQ : WBA Walgreens Boots Alliance Inc

Rule One Scores

MOAT: Compound Growth Rate

	10 Years	7 Years	5 Years	3 Years	1 Year	Score
Book Value + Dividend + Buy Backs Growth	10.5%	5.8%	3.3%	2.9%	-5.7%	30
Earnings Growth						
Total Revenue Growth	6.8%	2.5%	1.1%	4.5%	4.9%	13
Operating Cash Flow Growth	-6.2%	-16.3%	-22.0%	-25.6%	-42.1%	0
Free Cash Flow Growth	-26.6%	-42.2%	-54.1%	-67.5%	-93.5%	0
Rule One Moat Score						13

Management: Average Rate Of Return

	10 Years	7 Years	5 Years	3 Years	1 Year	Score
Return On Equity	10.5%	9.4%	6.4%	4.2%	-15.4%	50
Return On Invested Capital	7.2%	6.5%	4.4%	3.1%	-10.9%	25
Return On Assets	4.4%	3.5%	2.2%	1.6%	-5.3%	0
Net Debt to Earnings					2.71 Years	0
Net Debt to Free Cash Flow					59.11 Years	0
Rule One Management Score						15

When to Sell

Warren Buffett once remarked, "the best time to sell a wonderful business is never." This is because he owns part of or the entire company and retains control over its cash flow. As small investors we, too, would like to buy great companies on sale and keep them forever. But when the story changes and the company is no longer wonderful, we do have the advantage of getting out of the market in seconds, not like Warren Buffett or other institutional investors, who take 6 to 12 weeks to sell or buy into a company.

There are three scenarios when we might want to sell our stocks.

The first one is when we need the money. Planning for the future is crucial, ensuring that, when the day comes to sell, you have a range of options without significantly impacting your overall net worth. Anticipating this need allows you to select the businesses with the highest prices relative to their value, preventing forced sales during market downturns. Many retirees utilize their dividends to live on, but those who do not receive dividend income need to sell some of their stocks to live on.

The second reason to sell is when the fundamentals of a once-wonderful company have changed, and it is no longer a wonderful company. Industries and businesses can evolve, losing their appeal due to technological advancements or other factors. Vigilance over the Big Five—industry and business fundamentals, return on invested capital (ROIC), equity, cash flow, and debt—is essential. Any slippage in these areas, especially a decline in ROIC, serves as a red flag, indicating a potential need to exit. Use the Rule One toolbox to help you determine these numbers. Warren Buffett reminds us that, if a business no longer aligns with your understanding or violates fundamental principles, it may be time to exit. Don't wait hoping the price will go back up—sell, and take the loss.

The third time we would sell is when the market price significantly exceeds the Sticker Price (retail value). While the initial approach involves buying at a low price, selling occurs when the price surpasses the Sticker Price (companies' intrinsic value price) by 20 percent. This strategy takes advantage of market euphoria, allowing you to potentially repurchase the business at a discount within a year or two, as Mr. Market's exuberance tends to be short-lived.

The decision to sell when the price is 20% above intrinsic value is based on growth rate. If the company has a strong growth rate, such as 15% a year. It may be wise just to hold the company and not sell. But if the company is growing at only 4%, then selling the company may be a good idea. Phil

Town has said some of the biggest errors he has made is getting out of great companies too early.

Three of the greatest investors of all time, Warren Buffett, Jack Bogle, and Peter Lynch believe that, as long as the company continues to be wonderful, you never sell. You must be prepared financially and psychologically to hold them through thick and thin.

Why We Invest in the Stock Market

The stock market will give you the best return on any investment. Over the past 200 years, the stock market has returned more than 1000 times better than any other investment, including real estate, bonds, treasury bills, gold, or the US dollar. This book will show you how to maximize your investment in the stock market.

At the beginning of the annual Berkshire Hathaway meeting in 2018, Warren Buffett wanted to share an important lesson with its shareholders. I will summarize what he said: *"Let's look back to 1942 when I bought my first stock and all the things that have happened since that time. We have had fourteen presidents, seven Republicans and seven Democrats. We had world wars, 9/11, Cuban missile crisis, and all kinds of terrible events that affected the market. But the best single thing you could have done on March 11, 1942, when I bought my first stock was to buy an index fund (Buffett specifically mentioned the S&P 500 index fund) and never, ever look at another headline. Just like you would have bought a farm and let the tenant farmer run it for you and never sell it. If you had put in $10,000 in an index fund at that time and reinvested the dividends, you would have $51 million today in 2018.*

"If you took the same $10,000 and bought 300 ounces of gold, you would have only about $400,000 today. Gold does not produce anything, but businesses do. All you needed to do was to believe America would win the war and America would progress as it has ever since 1776. As America moves forward, American business moves forward. You didn't have to worry what stock to buy or what day to get in or out of the market or what the federal reserve would say. You just had to know that America works!"

Warren Buffett recommends for those amateur investors who do not want to spend the necessary time researching companies, just buy a very low-cost S&P 500 index fund every year through thick or thin. **Do not try to time the market but invest a specific amount routinely each month and never look**

back. A good example of this is the Charles Schwab S&P 500 Index Fund: (SWPPX) which has a very low total expense ratio of only 0.02%, with no minimum initial investment. One advantage of the S&P 500 is that, each year, they get rid of the bad companies and add newer companies that perform well.

Buffet is not a fan of cost-dollar averaging and recommends waiting for dips in the market, focusing on times when the stock or the S&P 500 is near 52-week lows. The S&P 500 was at its all-time high in July 2024. During market highs, keep the extra cash you add each month to your investment account into a money market accounts, such as Schwab's Value Advantage Money Fund—Investor Shares SWVXX paying around 5% today. This is even better than getting 2% or 3% in a dividend stock or the 1.5% you get in the dividend of S&P 500. To help you find the right time to invest, use the three-monthly indicators in the Charles Schwab *thinkorswim* trading platform.

Some investors want to equally distribute their cash over the three major indices such as the Dow Jones, NASDAQ, and S&P 500. Below is a chart showing their total return over different time periods.

Total returns over different time periods using Seekingalpha.com					
June 2024	One Year	Three-Year	Five Years	10 Years	Maximum
NASDAQ	30.7%	37.7%	161%	388%	729%
S&P 500	25%	26.7%	86.3%	172%	1,039%
Dow Jones	15.6%	12.3%	50.9%	131%	947%

Over the last 100 years, ending in December 2023, the average yearly return of the S&P 500 is 10.54%. This assumes dividends are reinvested. Dividends account for about 40% of the total gain over this period. Adjusted for inflation, the 100-year average stock market return (including dividends) is 7.4%. **One problem with this philosophy is that if you start late and only have 15 years before retirement, it's not that easy through index investing to reach true financial freedom. This is when Rule One investing is very important.**

Another problem that is overlooked with index investing is that there are times when the S&P 500 does not go up at all for many years. These are called "long-term bear markets." The good news is that these bear markets are the best times for value investors to get great buys on wonderful companies through the Rule One investing philosophy.

Stock Cycles

Michael Alexander wrote a book entitled *Stock Cycles*. He reviews the markets over 200 years of American history until the year 2000. During that time, we have had seven long-term bear and seven long-term bull markets. The total average real return in a long-term bull market was 13.2%, while the average return in a long-term bear market was 0.3%.

For example, from 1929 to 1955 (25 years) it went up only 1.5%. From 1966 to 1982, the total real return was a negative 1.5%. But from 1982 to the year 2000, the average total real return of the market was 14.8%. Alexander then went on to correctly predict that, starting in 2000, there would be a long-term bear market. In March 2013, the price of the Standard & Poor's (S&P) 500 was $1,527 the same price as it was in March 2000, resulting in no growth of the stock, which is why those 12 years are called "the lost decade."

From January 2011 up until January 2022, the S&P 500 average annual growth was about 14.5%, with reinvestment of dividends. In 2022, the S&P 500 dropped 18.11%, with dividends reinvested. This may have been an indication of the start of a brand-new bear market. From January 2022 until January 2024, the return on the S&P 500 has been flat at an annualized return (Dividends Reinvested) of 1.7%.

Remember, no one can predict the market's direction. The Rule One investment strategy is about making great returns whether the market is going up, down or sideways. Long-term bear markets are the ideal landscape for Rule One investors. These are the times when Rule One investors and Warren Buffett make the most money.

Buffett once said: "Every decade or so, dark clouds will fill the economic skies, and they will **briefly** rain GOLD. When this occurs, it's imperative that we rush outdoors carrying washtubs, not teaspoons."

There is a lot of talk about a new recession. One indication of recession has been the recent inversion of the yield curve, when long-term interest rates drop below short-term rates, indicating that investors are moving money away from short-term bonds and into long-term ones. This suggests that the market is becoming more pessimistic about the economic prospects for the near future.

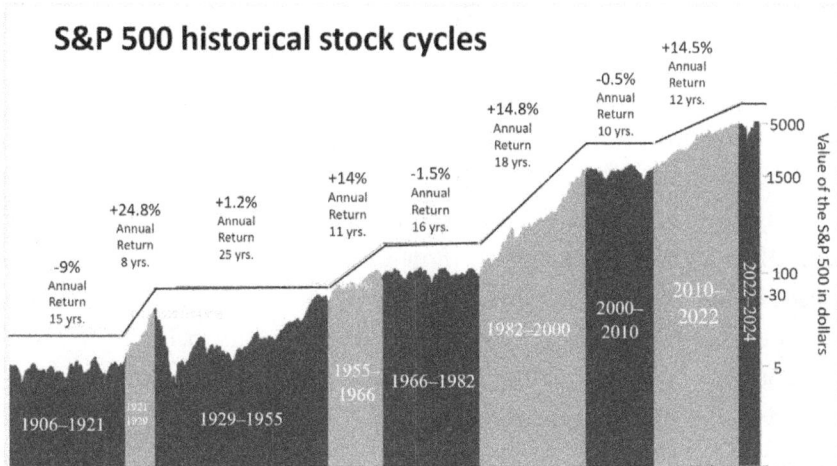

S&P 500 historical stock cycles

There are three other indicators that show the market is overvalued and that we may be in the beginning of a long, new-term bear market. These are the Buffett Indicator, the Shiller P/E ratio, and the Wilshire GDP. As of July 2024, the Buffett Indicator value is 195%, approximately (or about 2.0 standard deviations) above the historical trend line, suggesting that the stock market is strongly overvalued relative to GDP. Dr. Shiller states that, when the P/E ratio of the S&P 500 is low (below 10), the market is undervalued. When the P/E ratio is above 20, the market is overvalued. In July 2024, the Shiller P/E ratio for the S&P 500 stands at 36.3, and the Wilshire GDP today is above 195% (extremely overvalued).

All the above is very interesting, but making investment decisions based on economic predictions is incredibly difficult. Jack Bogle said, "Buy right and hold tight." Instead, focus on the underlying fundamentals of the company. Do your research on the companies of interest, make a watch list, wait, and buy when they go on sale and hold them. Over the long run, the fundamentals are ultimately all that truly matter. Time in the market is more important than timing the market.

One of the great investors of all time, Peter Lynch, said: "It is futile and impossible to try to predict the stock market, interest rates, or the

economy. If you spend 13 minutes a year on economics you've wasted 10 minutes."

Long-term bear markets can be devastating for retirees, who no longer work and rely on their income from their stock portfolio. The great advantage of owning strong dividend-growth companies is that their income will increase every year no matter how badly the stock or the stock market performs. This is one of the main reasons for owning strong dividend-growth companies that will rebound during market events. But always remember that we must be vigilant and continue to evaluate the statistics and fundamentals of the companies we own. We keep only those that are truly wonderful. When the price of wonderful companies is down, that is the time we buy more.

Bear markets also affect anyone who passively puts their money in the S&P 500 or any mutual fund that matches the market index. But long-term bear markets are ideal for Rule One investors. During this time, there are many big ups and downs in the market, during which you can buy great companies significantly undervalued. In the last long bear market, from 2000 to 2010, the market had two significant drops of 40% and 49%.

At the end of the long bear market in 2013, the price of the S&P 500 never got higher than the price it was in the year 2000. But during those 13 years, these were great opportunities for those who understood Rule One investing. In August 2007 Rule One investor Phil Town was interviewed on CNBC and recommended that we get out of the market. He used the three arrow indicators in *thinkorswim* to get out of the market in 2000 and 2007. These indicators also told him to get back in 2002, make an 87% return, and get out in 2007. Then he waited until 2009, when the three up-arrows told him to invest again, and, over the next three years, he had a return of 122%. See *thinkorswim* monthly graph below.

During this time, many wonderful companies' prices dropped in half. From 2009 to 2022, these same wonderful companies' prices grew more than 10 times. This is why it is so important to learn how to invest safely on your own in the stock market, identify wonderful companies, buy them when they are 50% below their intrinsic value, and keep them as long as they continue to be wonderful companies.

For those of you who do not want to worry about researching companies and getting greater returns, then just buy a S&P 500 mutual fund

S&P 500 return during the lost decade from 2000 to 2013 using thinkorswim 3 arrow indicators

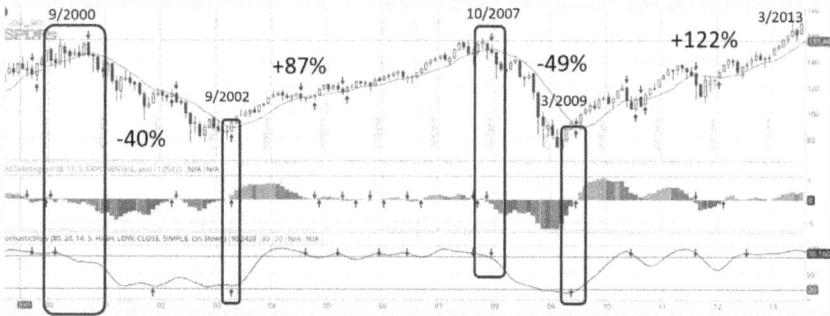

such as Schwab (SWPPX). The Charles Schwab *thinkorswim* trading platform, as seen above, it may be helpful to put your monthly investment allocations into the Schwab money market account (SWVXX) earning 5% when the S&P is at all-time highs and wait to invest in the S&P 500 index fund when it drops closer to its 52-week lows.

Where to Put Your Money Now

As of July 2024, the market is at its all-time high, and we have yet to have an event where we can buy great companies at half price. In order of preference, here are some suggestions.

Finish paying off debt, which will always give you the highest guaranteed return while you learn to paper trade in the market through *thinkorswim*.

Schwab money market account (SWVXX) is a good interim place for your money while you are waiting to get into the market. As of this writing, their annual return is about 5%. These are not FDIC insured, but they are SIPC insured up to $500,000. This fund is available for individual retirement and investment accounts. If your account is a corporation, a trust, or 401(k), then you would use either the Schwab Government Money Fund (SWVXX) or the Schwab Treasury Obligations Money Fund (SNOXX), also returning about 5%.

Warren Buffett doesn't like holding large amounts of cash and would rather be investing that money and using it to generate strong returns, however he also refuses to buy stocks unless prices are attractive. Today he believes the stock market is extremely overvalued, and he has $277 billion in cash. He is very happy to earn 5% on that money while he waits for stocks to go on sale.

Option trading: the goal in Rule One investing is to buy 6 to 15 wonderful companies at the right price. This may take some time when the market is at its all-time high, like it is today. Option trades are done over a 5-day to a 30-day period, allowing your money to be available for those events where you can buy your wonderful company at half price. To make money while you wait, you may want to learn to do option trading correctly. You need to have a good system, and this is best reviewed and discussed in the three-day virtual Zoom Rule One course.

Many option traders lose money because they have no system. In the Rule One Zoom course, you will learn specific rules to use for trading options that have been shown to have a 95% success rate, with a return of 15% to 30% a year. If done right, option trading can replace your income. As you practice paper trading, you will gain high confidence in the Rule One approach to option trading. **Once learned correctly many Rule One investors quit their day job and make a higher income option trading. This can be a life saver for retirees who have not saved well for retirement**.

These trades are done with wonderful companies that you want to own anyway. Rule One also offers a two-year advanced course with excellent instructors for those who want to expand their investing knowledge and learn more about step-by-step option trading. Here you can practice with paper money in your simulated *thinkorswim* trading account with no risk. In 2023, the Rule One study group did more than 120 real option trades with only one loss (99% success) and an annual return of more than 42%. It was a very good year.

Buy wonderful companies at half price. We must wait for an event to occur that pushes the stock to a half-price margin of safety level. This can happen when there is a company or market events and during volatile times, such as during a long bear market. Remember what Charlie Munger said: "**You make money in the stock market not when you buy or not when you sell but when you wait.**"

Retirement Accounts and Taxes

To count on having a comfortable life and a secure future in retirement, you must learn to invest on your own. This will ensure the maximum return on the money you have to invest. Passing on this responsibility to financial advisors to help you invest your savings could result in losing half or more of your retirement income.

The 5 common mistakes you need to avoid while planning for retirement

The **first** mistake is not understanding how much you're going to need to retire. During retirement, you may have fewer expenses in some areas, but other areas, such as healthcare and travel, will increase. Also, inflation will affect the buying power of your nest egg. Check out the investment calculator at: https://www.ruleoneinvesting.com/investment-calculators/

The **second** mistake is not taking advantage of your employer 401(k) matching money. Don't invest any more than is matched. The **third** mistake is relying on fund managers and advisors who could take up to 70% of your return in fees over time. You have the tools you need to learn to invest on your own on the internet. The **fourth** mistake is over-diversifying in many companies through mutual or index funds. Warren Buffett says "Diversification is a protection against ignorance. It makes very little sense for those who know what they're doing." Focus on owning 6 to 15 individual wonderful companies that you understand and like. **But if you are not interested in learning how to invest on your own, then the S&P 500 as described above is your best choice**. The **fifth** mistake is not researching these companies thoroughly and failure to understand the true intrinsic value so that you can purchase them at their margin-of-safety price. In the three day Rule One Zoom course, they will teach you how to determine true intrinsic value and use the toolbox to find the correct purchase price.

Investing in great companies is the best hedge against inflation and can be the best and safest place to put your money to beat inflation. Over the past 20 years, the inflation rate has been around 2.8%. In 2022, we had the highest inflation rate in 40 years, spiking to 9%. In July 2024, the inflation rate was 3.3% with no indication that it would fully subside soon.

If we could just buy and hold, there wouldn't be a tax issue. But sooner or later, we will want to spend the money. The big advantage of using the *thinkorswim* tools and three-arrow indicators is to help us get in and out of the market, with the big guys allowing us to make money while reducing the chance of losing money. The problem is, when that money is in a taxable account, there can be long-term or short-term capital-gains taxes. If you plan to sell a company, try to hold it for at least a year and a day so that you will have long-term capital gains.

It is still better to make and keep your gains (profits) earned in the market and sell, even if you must pay taxes. The strongest lesson we learn from Rule One investing is that we can keep our excess money working for us through one-week to one-month option trading, but we will have to pay taxes. I would rather make 20 to 25% gains and pay taxes on it, versus making 0% and paying no taxes. Remember: when your cash is in a money-market account, you will still be paying taxes on the interest earned.

The best choice is to be in a tax-free environment. That is why I encourage putting as much of your money in tax-free or deferred tax- free vehicles such as simple IRAs, Roth IRAs, SEP IRAs, 401(k)s, and back-door Roth IRAs. Check out the different tax-deferred and tax-free options: https://www.ruleoneinvesting.com/blog/financial-control/investment -vehicles/. Here is another site: https://www.irs.gov/retirement-plans/cola -increases-for-dollar-limitations-on-benefits-and-contributions

Since I'm not a tax attorney or CPA, I'm not going to advise you about how to set up these plans. I will tell you I'm not a huge fan of most 401(k) plans that force you to invest in mutual funds. The only time a 401(k) is better than an IRA is when the company you work for matches at least 50 percent of the funds you put in there. In that case, take the free money, but put in only the amount they're going to match.

Tax Strategies to Help You Reduce or Eliminate All Your Taxes on Your Investments

Investors must pay taxes on their dividends, but how much they pay depends on their income and whether the dividends are qualified or ordinary. Some realty companies (REITs) that pay dividends are non-qualified, such as Getty Realty (GTY), and you pay your standard tax rate.

Qualified dividends receive more favorable tax treatment but must meet a few criteria. They must be issued by a U.S. corporation that is publicly traded on major exchanges and indices, such as S&P 500, Dow Jones, or NASDAQ. Most dividends from U.S. companies are qualified but only if you own the stock for more than 60 days during the 121-day period that begins 60 days before the ex-dividend date.

The ex-dividend date, otherwise called the ex-date, typically comes one or two business days ahead of the record date. The record date is the day on which the company checks its records to identify shareholders of the company. An investor must be listed on that date to be eligible for a dividend payout that quarter. Therefore, to be eligible for dividends, you must buy or own the stock at least one business day before the ex-dividend date.

The dividend payout date, also known as the pay or payable date, is the day on which a declared stock dividend is scheduled to be paid (mailed out) to eligible investors. This date can be up to a month after the ex-dividend date. To find these key dates for your individual companies, go to your Schwab account, and click on the stock symbol. To verify that you received your dividends, go to your Schwab account, and click "history" up on top. This will show you all your account transactions, including dividend payouts.

The tax rates for ordinary (non-qualified) dividends (typically those that are paid out from most common or preferred stocks) are the same rates as you pay on regular income, such as salary or wages. This ranges somewhere between 10% and 37% for the 2023 tax year, depending on your income. Income-tax and capital-gains rates change over time, but in recent years, capital-gains rates have been substantially lower.

Currently, the 2024 tax schedule for qualified dividends features only three levels:

Those who earn less than a sum of $47,025 annually or are in the 10% and 12% tax brackets pay no taxes on the dividend income. If your income is below $94,054 for a married couple filing jointly, you will probably not owe any taxes on your dividend income.

Single taxpayers earning more than $47,025 up to $518,900 and married couples filing jointly who earn from $94,054 up to $583,750 are in the 22%, 24%, and 32% tax brackets. They pay their taxes on dividends at only a 15% tax rate.

Individuals earning $518,901 or more and married couples earning more than $583,751 are in the 35% or 37% tax bracket. They will pay only 20% of their annual dividend income in taxes. When the taxes are paid, you will get a step-up basis by Schwab on those stocks where you reinvested your dividends.

There is an additional 3.8% Net Investment Income Tax (NIIT) on investment gains or income. The IRS uses the lowest figure of net investment income or the excess of the modified adjusted gross income (MAGI) that exceeds $200,000 for single filers, $250,000 for married filing jointly, and $125,000 for married filing separately to determine this tax.

This tax is assessed regardless of whether the dividends received are classified as qualified or ordinary. The Net Investment Income Tax is an additional 3.8% tax that applies to dividend income (as well as realized gains) and increases the effective total tax rate on dividends and other investment income.

Learn more about current tax rates: https://www.investopedia.com/articles/taxes/090116/how-are-qualified-and-nonqualified-dividends-taxed.asp

Yet, even with this surcharge, qualified dividends are taxed at significantly better rates versus regular income or short-term capital gains. That doesn't reduce the risk of investing in the stock, but it does offer the prospect of keeping more of your hard-earned gains for yourself.

When you are buying dividend stocks in your tax-deferred account, such as a 401(k), or conventional IRA, you do not pay taxes on your reinvested dividend income that year. Instead, you will pay taxes on your compounded gains once you start to withdraw money in your retirement. The great exception to this is if you are in a Roth IRA. Unlike a 401(k) or IRA, where your cash deposits into the account are made with pre-tax dollars, all your cash deposits into a Roth IRA account are made with after-tax dollars, and so you never pay income tax on withdrawals or gains made in the future.

Every year in February, Charles Schwab will send you a document called a "1099." They will also send a copy to the IRS. This 1099 will tell you how much dividend income you collected in the previous year, so that you can calculate your taxes on it. Again, be sure to consult with a tax professional (which I am not).

As an employer, you may want to start your own self-directed safe-harbor 401(k) plan through Charles Schwab. This also has a Roth component. The employees will be given a range of different low-cost funds, including a money-market fund. Employers and other senior employees can have the option to self-direct their investments. Charles Schwab will introduce you to a plan administrator, who will create the plan design and do the testing of the plan. The cost of setting up the plan and maintaining it ranges between $3000 and $6000 a year, depending on the number of employees. Call Schwab at 877 456-0777. If you are not happy with your high-fee, wealth-advisor-run plan, you can easily move it to a self-directed plan through Schwab. https://www.youtube.com/watch?v=W7oVm3RJw_0

Solo 401(k): If you are self-employed (one-person outfit, a freelancer, or an independent contractor) and don't employ others, you can have a solo 401(k), also known as an independent 401(k) plan. Couples running businesses together also qualify. You can contribute to your solo 401(k) as both employer and employee. For 2024, you can contribute a combined total of $69,000. If you're 50 or older, you can add another $7,500. You can choose between a traditional plan or a Roth plan. I highly recommend that you make it a Solo Roth 401(k). https://www.investopedia.com/ask/answers/100314/do-i-need-employer-set-401k-plan.asp

If you have money in a standard tax-deferred 401(k), you can convert all or part of the money into a Roth 401(k). When you do this, you will need to pay the tax on the money transferred at the end of the year when you receive your 1099. Would you rather pay the tax on $100,000 now or pay 50% tax on it as it grows to $3,000,000 in 20 years or $15,000,000 over the 30 years? This should not be a hard question to answer. Once your standard 401(k) is converted into a Roth 401(k), you will never pay any tax on the gains or withdrawal of the money.

Everyone should have a Roth IRA. If you make too much money for a Roth IRA, then open a standard IRA account, and fund the maximum allowable amount that year. Once funded into the account, you can then transfer that money into a backdoor Roth IRA and pay the taxes.

Roth IRAs are tax-free forever! You put the money in after you pay tax on it, and it grows inside the Roth tax-free, and then, when you retire and take it out, you never have to pay tax on the gains. Teach your children how to invest using Rule One philosophy as you help them open and learn how to invest in their own Roth IRA account.

Any online brokerage can help you set up a Roth IRA over the phone. It's easy and takes only a few minutes. This can also show you how to roll over a 401(k) that's no longer being matched by your employer. (Your accountant can help you determine which one is best for you, as well as how much you can allocate to it on an annual basis.)

Simple IRAs are also excellent. You can pack away a huge amount every year tax-free if you qualify. The key thing is to get the money into a tax-deferred or tax-free Roth account. Not all the money we have to invest will be able to be put in a tax-free account. Some of the money you're investing might be in a taxable account.

When you become debt free and have learned to invest through paper trading, you will create such an abundance, most of which will probably be in a taxable account. I don't mind being in the highest tax bracket because it means I'm making the most money. Nathan Winklepleck, CFA, has a YouTube video that talks about retiring early and paying no taxes. https://www.youtube.com/watch?v=e4ocpTaWNdU

Estate Planning and Asset Protection Checklist

Statistics show that, in 2023, about 25% of 18- to 54-year-olds have a will. 45% of people over the age of 55 have a will. 81% of people over the age of 72 have a will, and only 18% were living trusts. James, my dental assistant of 19 years, died suddenly from a heart attack while golfing at age 37 without a will and extensive assets. His estate will need to go through probate and all the time and expenses associated with that process.

We just do not know when things will happen. It is also very important to have power of attorney for finance and healthcare directives. When you are debt free and have investments, you need to protect and ensure they are passed down to your family with very little tax and no probate or attorney fees.

Without these items, there is a great possibility that if something happens to you and your spouse, your drunken brother will take over all the money, spend it, and throw your kids out on the street. Think about it. Without a revocable living trust, your estate will go into probate, which makes all your assets public and is very expensive and emotionally draining to your heirs.

It could take years before your estate is settled, thus depleting much of your estate's assets because they are going to attorney fees.

I was working with a thirty-four-year-old dentist who was married and had a little girl, and one more child on the way. I told him to go to his local attorney and get these estate-planning documents drawn up. He said he would. Six months later, he was coming with his wife and team to one of my seminars in Seattle. During the flight, the plane had a landing-gear issue, and they thought they would have to make a crash landing in Seattle. Fortunately, they got the gear down and landed safely. At the meeting, I asked him, "Don't you feel better now that you have your asset-protection plan in place?" He sheepishly said, "I will get those things done as soon as I get back."

Find a local attorney, and get these things done now:

- Durable power of attorney for healthcare

- Durable power of attorney for finances

- Living will

- Standard will

- Revocable living trust

For a less-expensive approach, you can also go to LegalZoom.com and set up a will and power of attorneys for as little as $200 with the help of their attorneys.

https://www.legalzoom.com/personal/estate-planning/estate-planning-bundle.

Make sure to update beneficiaries on all your banking and investment accounts. The beneficiaries get first claim, and those listed on the will are secondary. Create a trust, and put all your taxable personal investment accounts and home in the name of the trust.

Fill out a document locator that shows all of your assets, the location of all important documents, such as your wills, trusts, brokerage accounts, and passwords. List the names, phone numbers, and emails of all important people, such as your accountant, attorney, bankers, and friends. All this and other important information should be given to someone you trust, such as your spouse, parents, or siblings, in case something happens to you and/or your spouse. This will be an important document for your family. You can download a free document locator at: https://doctorace.com/resources/

Just buy cheap term life insurance that will cover you until you are debt free and have created a portfolio of investments that can give you and your family passive income for life.

Health Insurance is very important for financial security. An illness/sickness can destroy you and your financial well-being for a decade or more. Try to be under your parents' health insurance until you are at least 26 years old. Find a job that provides health insurance.

Final Thoughts

Learning to invest on your own and creating wealth is not complicated! First learn how to make more money in your work, and quickly pay off debt. During this time, create an automatic monthly savings plan for investing, and maximize your personal investments in a tax-free Roth environment. Put this into a Schwab money market (SWVXX) account paying 5% while you learn to invest. I wrote a book in June 2024 to help you through this process entitled: "The Big Little Book on Creating Personal and Financial Freedom"

Compare how you and your advisor have done with the S&P 500 over time. Go to: https://www.doctorace.com/resources/ and download the free Excel comparison sheet to see how your investments have done against the S&P 500 fund. If you have not done as well as the S&P 500, then you must learn to invest correctly on your own, following the Rule One investing strategy. Open a brokerage account through Charles Schwab, and download the *thinkorswim* trading platform to learn how to paper trade.

Read the books by Phil Town, and go to his website ruleoneinvesting. com to learn how to find wonderful companies. I highly recommend that you take their $97.00 three-day Zoom investment course.

Create a watch list of wonderful companies by using the stock scanner on the Rule One toolbox. These are the businesses you want to own and that you will buy if the price is right. Your watch list can contain more than 20 stocks. Eventually you will own the best 6 to 15 companies from your initial watch list.

When evaluating companies for your watch list, look for three things. The first and maybe the most important is return on invested capital (ROIC). This is the earnings of the capital divided by all capital in the company. We would like to see it at 20% or higher. The next is evaluating the company's debt. Ideally, we would like a company that has no debt or less than one year of debt. The last thing we look at is Cash Flow. This is determined by looking at the income statement. Free cash flow is determined by subtracting the operating cash flow from the capital expenditures. We want free cash flow of around 10% or higher.

Sit back and relax. Buy only companies that are on sale. You wait for an event either in the economy, industry, or in the company itself. You need to be patient. You make money when you wait. Always buy a stock at a big Margin of Safety. Buying low and selling when they're very high can make you wealthy.

Most of our investment time is just doing nothing and waiting for the right event. You need to look at your portfolio only once a month, when you have added money into your account to put into the 5% money-market account or to buy more stocks. Other than that, **you should not** be even thinking about your portfolio or what the market is doing. Warren Buffett once said, "Lethargy bordering on sloth remains the cornerstone of our investment style."

Whatever you decide to do, the most important thing is to just get started. You don't have to wait for a big downturn in the market. The sooner you start investing in dividend stocks or a 5% money-market fund, the sooner you will start building wealth and creating passive income. Time is the greatest advantage that you can have in the stock market. If you combine compounding with time, you have the perfect recipe for building generational wealth.

www.ingramcontent.com/pod-product-compliance
Lightning Source LLC
Chambersburg PA
CBHW031910200326
41597CB00012B/573